GO!

A 30 – Day Devotional for Teens and Young Adults that are embarking on a new or renewed relationship with Jesus Christ

Kristin D. Hemingway

CreateSpace Publishing

Copyright © Kristin D. Hemingway, 2018
Published by CreateSpace, 2018

The right of Kristin D. Hemingway to be identified as the Author of the Work has been asserted by her in accordance with the Copyright, Designs and Patents Act 1988.

All rights reserved.

This book is sold subject to the condition it shall not, by way of trade or otherwise, be circulated in any form or by any means, electronic or otherwise without the author's prior consent, except for the use of brief quotations in a book review.

Printed in the United States of America

First Printing, 2018

Kristin Hemingway
www.Kristinhemingway.com

Dedication

To Mommy,

There is no me without you. Thank you for always encouraging me to find my voice and go my own way, even when you didn't agree with the path. I am who I am because of who you are to me!

To My Family, Spiritual Leaders, and the Friends That Became Family,

Thank you for encouraging my hunger for God and my expression of His gifts. Thank you.

To All of the Young People That I Have Had the Privilege of Leading,

Thank you for challenging me, inspiring me, pushing me, laughing with me, and encouraging me to share my gifts with the world. I love you more than words can express and I am still praying God's absolute best for your life.

Day 1 – Welcome to the Family

Congratulations! Today, or recently, you have decided to embark on what is sure to be the most amazing, rewarding and challenging adventure of your life. It is not an easy decision to choose to follow Jesus, but it is definitely a decision that is worth it.

In an instant, EVERYTHING has changed with this decision. The Bible tells us that we become new creations when we accept Jesus Christ. The old you is gone and the new you is here to stay (2 Corinthians 5:17). You may not feel any differently but know that your life is forever changed by the decision that you have just made.

Also, with this decision know that NOTHING has changed. Wait a minute, I know that I just said that everything has changed, and that is absolutely true, but at the same time nothing has changed. Most people won't notice anything different about you when you walk out of church today. You look the same, you sound the same, you are going back to school with the same grades and the same friends. You are going home to the same family and the same challenges that you had when you left this morning. This is because the changes that are taking place right now are starting on the inside of you.

As you learn more about God and build your relationship with Jesus, you will start to notice that you are changing, and because it's a change that takes place from the inside out, it may be hard for other people to notice it first. It will start with the way that you think about things and that will begin to change your behavior. As your thinking and behavior changes, your entire outlook on life will change. Your ability to navigate the challenges and deal with the difficult people and situations in your life will increase. You'll begin to understand that you are not facing them alone, but that you are facing them with a Lord and Savior that loves you and is by your side, guiding you along the way. And in the end, it won't be easy, but you will make it through.

So again, congratulations and WELCOME! You have made a decision to join the Family of Christ, and it is sure to be the best decision of your life!

JOURNAL: Take a minute to reflect on how you feel in this moment. Are you excited? Nervous? Scared? Hopeful? What made you accept Christ today? What are you most looking forward to in this new journey? What is the thing that you're not so excited about? Who are the people that are supporting you on this journey?

Day 2 – Building Relationship with God

How did your best friend become your best friend? It probably involved lots of communication and time together. The same is true for your relationship with Jesus. You will get to know and build a relationship with Him through spending time with Him and talking to Him. And the way that we talk to God is through prayer. In the Bible, Jesus gives us a model in how to have this conversation with God that is known as The Lord's Prayer.

Matthew 6:9-13 Living Bible (TLB)
9 "Pray along these lines: 'Our Father in heaven, we honor your holy name. 10 We ask that your kingdom will come now. May your will be done here on earth, just as it is in heaven. 11 Give us our food again today, as usual, 12 and forgive us our sins, just as we have forgiven those who have sinned against us. 13 Don't bring us into temptation, but deliver us from the Evil One.[a] Amen.'

CHALLENGE: Commit to memorizing The Lord's Prayer this week. Practice it every day and let it serve as a guide for how you begin your conversations with Jesus.

NOTE: Your personal prayers don't have to be long, use certain language, or sound a certain way. Prayer is simply a conversation between you and Jesus. It can take place anywhere that you are. You can say them out loud, write them down, or hold the conversation in your mind. Sometimes you share, sometimes you listen. The most important thing to do is to make sure that you communicate with the Lord daily. God wants you to feel comfortable sharing everything with Him because He wants you to know that He's there for you always, in all ways!

Day 3: You for Me, and Me for You

We are not meant to experience the Christian journey alone. God wants us to be a part of the community of believers as we go through this adventure. The Bible tells us that when two or three are gathered in the name of Jesus, he is sure to join them (Matthew 18:20). So who is your Christian community? Who are the people that you can share honestly with about your Christian journey? Who are the people that can pray with and for you? Who are the people that will help you stay on track? Who are the people that you can laugh and have fun with in a way that honors God?

Below, write the names of at least 5 people you can talk to that will help you to focus on your relationship with God. Don't forget to include your youth leader.

1. _____
2. _____
3. _____
4. _____
5. _____

Now, reach out to each of these people and thank them for joining you on the journey. A Christian experience lived out in strong community is a true gift from God! It makes the brighter days brighter and the sad days lighter. Enjoy your time as you build your Christian community.

Day 4: Reading the Word

An important part of your Christian journey will be building a daily practice of reading the Bible. In this process, it is important to have a Bible that you are comfortable using and that you can understand fairly easily. A teen study Bible is always a good choice as it will offer you extra information that will help you to understand what's happening in the scriptures. If you are feeling a bit overwhelmed by the process ask your youth leader or other members of your Christian community for help. They would love to help you select the right Bible to help you to successfully navigate your Christian journey.

In the meantime, download a Bible app, like YouVersion, so that you can always have it with you. They have several study plans that you can try out to help you learn more about a specific book of the Bible or a topic that interest you. It will also allow you to read the scripture in several different versions to aid you in understanding what the Bible is saying.

CHALLENGE: Make a practice of reading the Bible every day. Studies prove that it takes 21 days to form a new habit, so over the next 21 days commit to reading the book of John in the New Testament. Read one chapter a day and find joy in learning more about who Jesus was and is and how that impacts your life today.

JOHN 1 – Reflections

WORDS/PHRASES THAT STOOD OUT TO ME

_____

_____

_____

_____

THINGS I WANT TO STUDY MORE

_____

_____

_____

_____

CENTRAL POINT/THEME

_____

_____

_____

ONE TAKEAWAY TO APPLY TO MY LIFE

_____

_____

_____

_____

Day 5: Running Your Race

Many people end up frustrated in their Christian journey because they find themselves trying to make their Christian journey like someone else's instead of embracing the road that God has before them. It is okay to learn from other people on this adventure, but we do ourselves a huge disservice if we try to make our journey become a mirror image of theirs. The Bible tells us that we need to run our own race and focus on Jesus and not others in our process (Hebrews 12:1-3).

Have you found yourself comparing your Christian journey to other people around you? How has that made you feel? Take a moment to pray and ask God to show you what He wants you to focus on in your journey. When you're finished praying, use the lines below to write what you believe that God is showing you that He wants you to focus on in this beginning part of your Christian journey. Then write the first three things that you can do to help make progress in that area of your life.

FOCUS:
_____

Step 1:
_____

Step 2:
_____

Step 3:
_____

JOHN 2 – Reflections

WORDS/PHRASES THAT STOOD OUT TO ME

_____
_____
_____
_____

THINGS I WANT TO STUDY MORE

_____
_____
_____
_____

CENTRAL POINT/THEME

_____
_____
_____
_____

ONE TAKEAWAY TO APPLY TO MY LIFE

_____
_____
_____
_____

Day 6: Service to Humanity

As a part of our Christian journey God is calling us to service both in His church and in the world. In Matthew 25, Jesus talks about being hungry, thirsty, sick, imprisoned, a stranger and more. He celebrates those that took care of His needs and welcomed Him. These people had never laid eyes on Jesus and were confused by His celebration of them. He told them that by serving those that they found in need they had actually served Him.

Jesus calls us to a life of not just focusing on our own needs, but of training our eyes to see and meet those that are most vulnerable around us. This could be sharing our lunch with a classmate that may not have the means to get their own, volunteering our time to tutor kids that are struggling academically, or helping our Mom bring the groceries in. The point is that as followers of Jesus, we all need to train our eyes to see the needs of those around us and then we need to train our hearts to respond to them.

CHALLENGE: Today take a moment and pray for God to show you the needs around you that He wants you to meet, and then go and meet them. It could be as simple as helping a teacher organize papers in their classroom, buying food for a stranger, or taking on extra chores around the house. Whatever it may be, open your eyes and your heart to serve the needs of those God brings to your attention. Write about your experience below.

_____
_____
_____
_____

JOHN 3 – Reflections

WORDS/PHRASES THAT STOOD OUT TO ME

_____
_____
_____
_____
_____

THINGS I WANT TO STUDY MORE

_____
_____
_____
_____
_____

CENTRAL POINT/THEME

_____
_____
_____
_____
_____

ONE TAKEAWAY TO APPLY TO MY LIFE

_____
_____
_____
_____
_____

Day 7: I Give Myself Away

As a member of the Christian family, Christ expects you to share what you have been blessed with, with those around you. For many of us this includes the concept of tithing or giving a tenth of your financial resources back to support the work of the church in your community. But it doesn't just stop at sharing your financial resources. God has also given you gifts and talents that He wants you to share with the Body of Christ as well. In Christian community we all have a role to play, and when someone doesn't show up to do their part the entire body suffers because each part is necessary! Every gift is important! Read 1 Corinthians 12 to learn more about spiritual gifts and how we are all one body.

CHALLENGE: Memorize 1 Corinthians 12:26-27

Today, think of the ways that you can give your time, talent, and treasure to the church body. We need everyone on the team to play their role so that we can be successful with the mission that God has given us in the world.

TIME --

_____

TALENT --

_____

TREASURE --

_____

JOHN 4 – Reflections

WORDS/PHRASES THAT STOOD OUT TO ME

_____
_____
_____
_____
_____

THINGS I WANT TO STUDY MORE

_____
_____
_____
_____
_____

CENTRAL POINT/THEME

_____
_____
_____
_____
_____

ONE TAKEAWAY TO APPLY TO MY LIFE

_____
_____
_____
_____
_____

Day 8: Meditation – Spending Time With God

One of the important aspects of being a Christian is learning to hear the voice of God so that we can learn to obey the voice of God. We all live in this world that has our days full of busyness and noise. Meditation is our personal effort to slow down the busyness, quiet the noise, and focus on God. When we meditate, we press pause on the activity in our life to give God our full and undivided attention. It allows us to focus on God's Word so that we can live out God's purpose in our lives like it's referenced in Joshua 1:8.

Meditation can feel difficult in the beginning if we are not used to slowing down and getting quiet, but if we do not give up, it can become a time of great peace and joy as we learn to hear the voice of God.

When we meditate, we choose to focus on a specific part of scripture and spend a specific period of time thinking on it and what God is trying to tell us through it. It can be a single word, a single line, paragraph or chapter of scripture. You can start with five minutes of focusing on it and it's meaning or you can spend one hour contemplating what God is trying to say to you. The amount of time does not matter, but consistently participating in the act of meditation does.

CHALLENGE: Take the following scripture and spend five minutes contemplating what God is trying to tell you through it. Write a few of your thoughts below. You can choose to focus on one word, a short phrase, or the entire scripture. The key is to place your focus on it for the next five minutes. Turn the word or words around in your head. Say them with your mouth. Add your name in there to make it personal. Take your time with it, and see what God wants to reveal to you so that you can then do what He wants you to do.

Matthew 22:37-38 Common English Bible (CEB): He replied, *"You must love the Lord your God with all your heart, with all your being,*[c] and with all your mind. ³⁸ This is the first and greatest commandment.

JOHN 5 – Reflections

WORDS/PHRASES THAT STOOD OUT TO ME

THINGS I WANT TO STUDY MORE

CENTRAL POINT/THEME

ONE TAKEAWAY TO APPLY TO MY LIFE

Day 9: Sacrificing for Growth

Fasting is the act of giving something up or sacrificing for spiritual purposes. Many people instantly think of food when they think of fasting, but you can fast from anything, within reason, that could be a distraction from your relationship with God. Fasting can be for a few hours, or it can go on for many days. However long you choose to fast, it is most important that you fill the time that you now have available to you with something that will strengthen your relationship with God. We see many people do many different types of fasts for various days throughout the Bible. Daniel fasted as he prepared for service to the King, Esther and the entire Jewish community fasted to save them from death. Nehemiah fasted before asking for permission to rebuild Jerusalem. And the list goes on and on.

CHALLENGE: Take a moment to think about something that may be distracting you as you are building your new relationship with God. Take this opportunity to give that thing up for 24 hours and refocus your attention on something that will strengthen your relationship with God for that period of time. If you're not sure what to do during this time, take this as an opportunity to look up scriptures that help you to understand more about fasting. You can fast from eating, social media, playing video games, etc. Write down a few thoughts on your experience below.

I am fasting from _____

What I noticed during my fast

_____

_____

_____

_____

JOHN 6 – Reflections

WORDS/PHRASES THAT STOOD OUT TO ME

_____
_____
_____
_____
_____

THINGS I WANT TO STUDY MORE

_____
_____
_____
_____
_____

CENTRAL POINT/THEME

_____
_____
_____
_____
_____

ONE TAKEAWAY TO APPLY TO MY LIFE

_____
_____
_____
_____
_____

Day 10: Worshipping Every Day and in Every Way

In Romans 12:1-2, we are called by God to live a life of worshipping Him. The author of Romans calls us choosing to dedicate our lives to worshiping God our reasonable sacrifice. Many people do not understand what it means to worship God with their everyday life.

Here a few thoughts that will help you to understand what that could look like for you. First, understand that worship is not a single act or a particular moment, but it is a complete lifestyle. Committing to living a life of worship means that we are committed to honoring God with everything that we do in our lives. You may be wondering how that is even possible. Well it starts with pausing to ask yourself the question, "If I do this, will it push me closer to God or will it move me further away?" When we center our actions on making sure that everything that we do will honor God and push us closer to Him, we are focusing on living lives of worship. When we make bringing God glory our central focus, we can know that we are living a life that is centered on worshipping the one that created us.

What is one thing you can do today, or one thing that you can stop doing today to bring God glory?

_____

_____

JOHN 7 – Reflections

WORDS/PHRASES THAT STOOD OUT TO ME

_____
_____
_____
_____
_____

THINGS I WANT TO STUDY MORE

_____
_____

_____
_____

CENTRAL POINT/THEME

_____
_____
_____
_____

ONE TAKEAWAY TO APPLY TO MY LIFE

_____
_____
_____
_____
_____

Day 11: Being Alone Together

Think of your strongest relationships with the people in your life. Odds are that over the course of knowing each other you have had significant moments between just the two of you that helped to create the unbreakable bond that you share. Your one-on-one conversations, shared memories, special traditions, and inside jokes have enabled you to create a special relationship that you know you can always count on. Well guess what, God wants that type of relationship with you. He wants special time with just the two of you where you get to know Him better, share your secrets with Him, listen to what He wants to share with you. He wants an opportunity to create special memories and traditions.

Solitude and silence are two things that we can use to create space for us to build this type of significant relationship with God. When we practice solitude, we make an intentional effort to separate ourselves from people and things for a moment, so that we can focus on growing in our relationship with Him. As we choose to practice solitude, we are also becoming more like Jesus. The Bible offers us several scriptures to show that Jesus often withdrew from the crowds to spend time alone with the Father, like in Luke 5:16.

You can practice solitude in small ways every single day by setting aside daily time in your life to focus specifically on your relationship with God. In addition, you should also practice having longer periods of solitude at least once a month where you take up to an entire day to focus on building your relationship with God. This doesn't mean that you have to spend your day avoiding people altogether, but it does mean that you spend your day focusing on spending time in communion and conversation with God in everything that you do.

CHALLENGE: Today, take at least one hour where you completely disconnect from the world so that you can connect with God. Spend time worshipping with song, praying, meditating, listening, and just enjoying His company. If the weather allows, spend some of that time with God in nature and see what you can learn from this experience.

BONUS: Pick a day and spend at least 4 hours in solitude. During that time journal what you believe God is saying to you throughout the experience of intentionally focusing on spending time with Him!

JOHN 8 – Reflections

WORDS/PHRASES THAT STOOD OUT TO ME

_____
_____
_____
_____

THINGS I WANT TO STUDY MORE

_____
_____
_____
_____

CENTRAL POINT/THEME

_____
_____
_____
_____

ONE TAKEAWAY TO APPLY TO MY LIFE

_____
_____
_____
_____

Day 12: A New Creation

Have you ever wanted to get a fresh start? When we accept Christ, the Bible tells us that we become a new creation. That's what it means to be born again. It's our opportunity to have a fresh start and to become the best person that we can possibly be. If you were known for having a bad attitude, here is your opportunity to develop a new one. If you were mean to your siblings before, here is your opportunity to become a life of practicing kindness. If you weren't the best student in the past, here's your chance to be on the honor roll. All things are made new in Christ.

Read 2 Corinthians 5:17. Below list 1-2 areas of your life that you are going to take advantage of this opportunity to say good-bye to the past and have a fresh start. Write what it looks like now, and how it will look after you begin again.

1. _____
   _____
   _____

2. _____
   _____
   _____

CHALLENGE: Memorize 2 Corinthians 5:17, and when the old you tries to crop up, remind yourself that you were made new in Christ by reciting this scripture.

JOHN 9 – Reflections

WORDS/PHRASES THAT STOOD OUT TO ME

THINGS I WANT TO STUDY MORE

CENTRAL POINT/THEME

ONE TAKEAWAY TO APPLY TO MY LIFE

Day 13: Prayer the Changes Things

When you look around your community, do you notice the problems that are going unsolved? Have you ever wondered who was responsible for making things right? Well the answer is YOU, and all of us as Christians. And that answer begins with prayer. The Bible tells us in 2 Chronicles 7:14, " if my people who belong to me will humbly pray, seek my face, and turn from their wicked ways, then I will hear from heaven, forgive their sin, and heal their land."

God is waiting on us to heal our land. We are His hands and feet and we start the journey of seeing our communities made whole by spending time praying for the things that we see need to be addressed in order for people to thrive.

CHALLENGE: Take some time to identify 1-2 issue(s) in your community that need to be addressed and for the next week, pray for them every day. Pray for God to give you insight and wisdom so that you can see how He wants you to get involved in making things better. Make sure to make a note of what God is sharing with you so that you have a road map to seeing change happen in your community.

1. _____
   _____
2. _____
   _____

JOHN 10 – Reflections

WORDS/PHRASES THAT STOOD OUT TO ME

THINGS I WANT TO STUDY MORE

CENTRAL POINT/THEME

ONE TAKEAWAY TO APPLY TO MY LIFE

Day 14: Life Long Learner

You are now at least two weeks into your Christian journey and hopefully you are having an amazing time of learning and growth. The reality is though, that there is some stuff that you may feel like you're getting wrong. There is so much to learn as we embark on a relationship with Jesus that it can sometimes be overwhelming when we are just getting started. Here's the thing, just like you don't know everything that you need to know on the first day of school to do well in the class, you won't learn everything that you need to learn about how to live this Christian life in a couple of days.

It takes ongoing study of God's Word, and by ongoing, we mean the rest of your life. There is always something new to discover and that is why it's important for us to keep reading and meditating on God's Word regardless of where we are in our Christian journey. We will never know enough to not require study. In addition, studying God's Word helps us to maintain peace and hope when life gets difficult. Romans 15:4 tells us how all scriptures were written for us to learn from and to give us hope as we walk out this faith journey.

CHALLENGE:

1. Read Romans 15:4.
2. Think of something that you have wondered about God's perspective on.
3. Try to find 1-2 Scriptures that relate to it.
4. Journal about how finding out God's perspective made you feel.

NOTE: *If you have trouble finding a scripture that relates to the topic that you're wondering about, reach out to a member of your community that you identified on Day 3 and see if they can help you.*

JOHN 11 – Reflections

WORDS/PHRASES THAT STOOD OUT TO ME

_____
_____
_____
_____
_____

THINGS I WANT TO STUDY MORE

_____
_____
_____
_____
_____

CENTRAL POINT/THEME

_____
_____
_____
_____
_____

ONE TAKEAWAY TO APPLY TO MY LIFE

_____
_____
_____
_____
_____

Day 15: Purposeful Living

Did you know that God has already planned the good things that He wants you to do? He knew that you would give your life to Christ and when. He made you with your unique set of gifts talents and abilities, and as a result the Bible tells He made you intentionally do the work that He knew that you would be called to do in this world.

Read Ephesians 2:8-10 and begin to think about what your purpose may be. Pray and ask God to show you what you're naturally good at, what you're interested in, and what the world needs. For many of us, it's at the place where these three things intersect that many of us have our purpose revealed.

Below right down what God shows you through prayer and what your initial thoughts may be.

_____
_____
_____
_____
_____
_____
_____
_____
_____
_____
_____
_____
_____
_____
_____
_____

JOHN 12 – Reflections

WORDS/PHRASES THAT STOOD OUT TO ME

_____
_____
_____
_____
_____

THINGS I WANT TO STUDY MORE

_____
_____
_____
_____
_____

CENTRAL POINT/THEME

_____
_____
_____
_____
_____

ONE TAKEAWAY TO APPLY TO MY LIFE

_____
_____
_____
_____
_____

Day 16: Renew Your Mind

Have you ever tried to change your behavior, but no matter what you tried you always ended up doing the same things? That's because it's hard to change our behavior without first changing the way that we think about things. This is why God tells us in Romans 12:1-2 to be transformed by the renewing of our mind. He's given us the blueprint for changing our outward actions and it starts with changing our inner thoughts.

Below, write one or two areas of your life where you need to change your thoughts so that you can change your behavior. Pray for God to show you His perspective and for Him to surround you with people that will encourage you as He is transforming you from the inside out.

CHALLENGE: If you have a cell phone, make Romans 12:1-2 your screensaver for the next week. If you don't have a cell phone, write it on a note card and carry it around with you for the next week to serve as a reminder that God is changing you from the inside out. Let Him change your thoughts so that your actions will follow.

JOHN 13 – Reflections

WORDS/PHRASES THAT STOOD OUT TO ME

_____
_____
_____
_____
_____

THINGS I WANT TO STUDY MORE

_____
_____
_____
_____
_____

CENTRAL POINT/THEME

ONE TAKEAWAY TO APPLY TO MY LIFE

Day 17: For Your Good

No matter where we are in life, one thing that we can all count on is that at some point someone will do something to hurt us, or we will have an experience that brings us some measure of emotional pain. We will experience loss, betrayal, disappointment, confusion or some other feeling that is less than enjoyable. When that happens, many people believe that is God punishing them, or that maybe it is a consequence for something that may have done previously, which is not always the case. Even when it is, the Bible lets us know that God can use all our experiences for our good.

Romans 8:28 says, "And we know that God causes everything to work together for the good of those who love God and are called according to his purpose for them." So here's the thing. This doesn't mean that everything that happens to feel good is good. It does mean that God is such a powerful God that He can take even the worst things in our lives and use them for our benefit.

Take this opportunity to think of a moment where something negative may have happened in your life. Really examine the experience and try to see where God used it to benefit you in some way. This is definitely a challenging task, but as we learn to train our hearts and minds to seek out where God has used our painful experiences for our long-term good, we will be better able to face the challenges that each day brings.

JOHN 14 – Reflections

WORDS/PHRASES THAT STOOD OUT TO ME

___

THINGS I WANT TO STUDY MORE

___

CENTRAL POINT/THEME

___

ONE TAKEAWAY TO APPLY TO MY LIFE

___

Day 18: Don't Worry, Be Happy

In the mid-80's there was a popular song entitled, "Don't Worry, Be Happy." In it, the singer exclaims, "In this life you'll have some trouble. When you worry, you make it double. Don't worry, be happy." Worry and happiness cannot coexist. It is not possible to constantly be going over all of the possible negative outcomes and to think that we will have happiness at the same time. Also, the Bible provides us with a solution for worrying. It doesn't just tell us not to worry, it tells us what we should do instead. In Philippians 4:6-7, we are told, " Don't worry about anything; instead, pray about everything. Tell God what you need, and thank Him for all He has done. Then you will experience God's peace, which exceeds anything we can understand. His peace will guard your hearts and minds as you live in Christ Jesus." Having a concern is normal, but we are not required to worry about anything. Because of our relationship with God, we are invited to share our concerns with Him and to know that He's got it, even if He doesn't always give us the answer that we want. Our reward for trusting Him is peace, and with peace we can have happiness.

Are you currently worrying about anything? If so, take this opportunity to present your worries to God and ask for your desired outcome in prayer. Whether or not you get exactly what you wanted in the end, you can be rest assured that God heard you and that He wants to give you His peace in exchange for your worry.

Life is quite challenging on its own. Let's choose to not make it doubly so by worrying and losing the peace that God promises us when we choose to present our concerns to Him instead of worrying about them.

CHALLENGE: Look up the words to the song "It Is Well With My Soul" and the history of its writer, Horatio G. Spafford. Does learning the history of this song make you view Philippians 4:6-7 differently? Does it make it easier or harder for you to face the challenges that you may be currently dealing with or have dealt with in the past? Share your thoughts below.

_____
_____
_____

JOHN 15 – Reflections

WORDS/PHRASES THAT STOOD OUT TO ME

_____
_____
_____
_____
_____

THINGS I WANT TO STUDY MORE

_____
_____
_____
_____
_____

CENTRAL POINT/THEME

_____
_____
_____
_____
_____

ONE TAKEAWAY TO APPLY TO MY LIFE

_____
_____
_____
_____
_____

Day 19: Seek First

Often times, in life we find ourselves concerned about and focusing on making sure that we have our needs met. Now, it is important to make sure that we have what we need to thrive, it is equally important that we do not let these thoughts consume us because it can and will take our focus off of pursuing God and what He has for us in any given season of our life. Take the time to read Matthew 6:25-33. Here is tells us that not only does God know exactly what we need, but He will be sure to give it to us. So the next time you find yourself overly concerned with whether or not you will have your needs met, remember what we are taught in Matthew 6.

CHALLENGE: Take a moment to memorize Matthew 6:33. Let it serve as your reminder to seek the Kingdom of God above else and trust that God will make sure that your needs are met in the process.

JOHN 16 – Reflections

WORDS/PHRASES THAT STOOD OUT TO ME

_____
_____
_____
_____
_____

THINGS I WANT TO STUDY MORE

_____
_____
_____
_____
_____

CENTRAL POINT/THEME

_____
_____

ONE TAKEAWAY TO APPLY TO MY LIFE

Day 20: Inseparable Love

Have you ever had a moment where you felt unlovable? Is there a decision that you've made or a habit that you have that you feel makes it harder for people to love the real you? Sometimes, it can be difficult to accept that God's love for us is all encompassing and never ending because the people in our lives have reminded us of how challenging we can be to love at times. In Romans 8, God tells us that there is NOTHING that can separate us from His love. There is nothing that we can think, say, or do that makes us unlovable to our creator.

Read Romans 8:37-38. How does it make you feel to know that there is literally NOTHING that can separate you from the love of God? Take a moment to write your initial thoughts below.

_____
_____
_____
_____
_____
_____
_____

JOHN 17 – Reflections

WORDS/PHRASES THAT STOOD OUT TO ME

_____
_____
_____
_____

THINGS I WANT TO STUDY MORE

_____
_____
_____

CENTRAL POINT/THEME

ONE TAKEAWAY TO APPLY TO MY LIFE

Day 21: Learning How To Love

Have you ever wondered what it means to really love someone? Like how do you know if you are loving them well, or even loving them at all? Some people believe that love is simply a feeling and it has no tangible checklist to prove that the feelings are real, but the Bible tells us something different. In 1 Corinthians 13:4-8, we are given a basic checklist for what love looks like. It's patient, it's not rude, it doesn't keep a record of wrongdoing, it last forever, and so much more.

Now take a moment to think about the people in your life that you love. Are you displaying these characteristics in your love for them? Do you see places where you can grow in how you love others? On the line below, write the attribute of love that you need to work on the most in this season. Pray that God help you to grow in that area so that you can learn to love those in your life in the best way possible.

I want to grow in love by growing in this area:
_____

JOHN 18 – Reflections

WORDS/PHRASES THAT STOOD OUT TO ME

_____
_____
_____
_____
_____

THINGS I WANT TO STUDY MORE

_____
_____
_____
_____
_____

CENTRAL POINT/THEME

ONE TAKEAWAY TO APPLY TO MY LIFE

Day 22: Your Heart's Orchard

One of the things that we are promised when we begin a new relationship with Christ is the Holy Spirit. The Holy Spirit serves as a guide for us on our Christian journey. The Holy Spirit is referenced as a friend, a comforter, a counselor, and so many other things. Unfortunately, many people choose not to access the power of the Holy Spirit in their life and as a result they miss out on the benefits, or fruit, that come out of developing a relationship with the Holy Spirit. They either feel as if they can get by without the Spirit, or they honestly feel like they don't know how and are too afraid to ask for help from a trusted friend or leader. As a result, they miss out on the benefits of this amazing relationship. Galatians 5:16 tells us that is to our benefit to let the Spirit guide our life, and later in the chapter, Galatians 5:22-23 tells us what we gain by allowing the Spirit to guide us.

Read Galatians 5:16-23. Identify 1-2 Fruits of the Spirit that you can see present in your life. Are you full of joy? Do you have a great amount of patience? Are you overflowing with love? Now take a moment to thank God for the fruit that is visible in your life.

Next, read Galatians 5:22-23 again. Identify 1-2 Fruits of the Spirit that you struggle with seeing in your life. Now, pray and ask God to help you grow in those areas. Ask Him to help you to live with the Holy Spirit as your guide so that all of the Fruits of the Spirit may be seen in your life.

The Fruits of the Spirit that are easily seen in my life are:

_____

The Fruits of the Spirit that I need help to develop are:

_____

JOHN 19 – Reflections

WORDS/PHRASES THAT STOOD OUT TO ME

_____
_____
_____
_____
_____

THINGS I WANT TO STUDY MORE

_____
_____
_____
_____
_____

CENTRAL POINT/THEME

_____
_____
_____
_____
_____

ONE TAKEAWAY TO APPLY TO MY LIFE

_____
_____
_____
_____
_____

Day 23: An Enduring Faith

As you progress through your faith journey, you will find that more often than you would like, both people and circumstances will come to test your faith. Maybe a long-time friend will say that they no longer want to be your friend because you've changed. Or maybe you will be presented with an opportunity to cheat on a test or to disobey your parents and do something that you know that they would not want you to do. Maybe the temptation is to experiment with drugs with your friend or to go too far in your dating relationship.

The truth is that we all face challenges of many kinds as we grow in our relationship with Jesus. Even still, sometimes it can feel as if we are being tempted because maybe we weren't serious when we accepted Christ as our Lord, but that couldn't be further from the truth.

James 1:2-4 tells us to find joy when our faith is tested because it means that we are being presented with an opportunity for our endurance to grow. And as our endurance grows and our faith is increased, we will be better equipped to face the next challenge that we are presented with.

What's an area in your life where you are being tested right now?

_____
_____
_____
_____

Pray that God will help you to increase your endurance so that you come out stronger on the other side and ready to face the next challenge that is to come.

JOHN 20 – Reflections

WORDS/PHRASES THAT STOOD OUT TO ME

THINGS I WANT TO STUDY MORE

CENTRAL POINT/THEME

ONE TAKEAWAY TO APPLY TO MY LIFE

Day 24: Pleasing God

As we go through our Christian journey, we are going to often encounter situations and circumstances that require us to believe God in new ways. Many times these circumstances will require us to exercise faith that we didn't even know that we had. And it's that faith that we need to possess to be pleasing to God. The funny thing is that many people will say that they don't know how to have faith, but the reality is that's not true. Most of us have exercised our faith our whole life through the practice of worry, and worry is simply misplaced faith. Worry is a faith that the negative will come to pass, even if we want to hope for the positive. So let's practice faith in the positive. Let's believe that God is who He says He is and that He can do what He said He can do.

Hebrews 11:1 gives us the definition of faith, and in Hebrews 11:6 we are told that it is impossible to please God without it.

Make sure that as you walk through your Christian journey that you focus on pleasing God by exhibiting great faith in every circumstance.

CHALLENGE: Memorize Hebrews 11:1 and Hebrews 11:6. Recite them to yourself when you see that your faith has been misdirected into worry. Let it help you refocus your mind and heart on believing God even in the most challenging of situations.

JOHN 21 – Reflections

WORDS/PHRASES THAT STOOD OUT TO ME

_____
_____
_____
_____
_____

THINGS I WANT TO STUDY MORE

_____
_____

CENTRAL POINT/THEME

ONE TAKEAWAY TO APPLY TO MY LIFE

Day 25: No Fear

Are you a person that deals with a lot of fears? I'll be the first to admit that this Christian journey can sometime be a pretty frightful one. It can be scary to think about following Christ and what that might mean for your life. There may be thoughts about you having to give up your dreams to do something weird and random for God. Or you might be scared that you will lose important relationships with friends and family members because you are being asked to live this different lifestyle. Whatever your fears may be, know that you are not alone. Everyone that has walked this Christian journey has had to face a fear or two as they made a decision to live their life with Christ instead of without Him.

The cool thing is that while God knows that we will face many scary moments, He still wants us to have no fear. He doesn't say this because the situations aren't scary either. He tells us to have no fear for one reason, and one reason alone, and that reason is because regardless of what we face, he promises to be with us! This truth is found in Isaiah 41:10.

FOCUS: Take some time today to meditate on this truth. Think about the places where you may be struggling with fear and think about them in light of what God says to us in Isaiah 41:10.

Day 26: Letting Go

Throughout our life we are going to encounter people and situations that inevitably break our heart and cause us pain. When that happens, many of us have a hard time forgiving the people responsible for our heartache pain. We feel that they owe us something, and we choose to hold that over their heads and punish them with it for as long as we can. However, that is not the life that God is calling us to.

Remember, we are constantly in the need of forgiveness for ourselves. Our entire salvation rest on being forgiven for the sins that we committed because of the work that Christ did on the cross. The reality is that He didn't just die so that we could be forgiven, He also died so that those who hurt us could be forgiven too.

Throughout the Bible God calls us to let go of the pain and hurt of the past and to forgive those that have hurt us, whether it was intentional or unintentional. In Matthew 18, when Peter asks how many times we should forgive someone for hurting us, it is recorded that Jesus said that we should forgive them seventy-seven times, or even more depending on the version of the Bible that you read. Both Matthew 6 and Luke 6 tells us that we have to forgive others in order to be forgiven. Ephesians 4 tells us that we show kindness and compassion through forgiving others, and the list of examples that tell us to forgive goes on.

CHALLENGE: Think of the people in your life that you need to forgive, and if need be, include yourself on that list. Take some time today and read over the scriptures that are listed and after reading them, pray that God help you to forgive those that have hurt you in your life.

Keep in mind that forgiveness is not a one time process. You will find yourself having to forgive people for the rest of your life, just like you will find yourself in need of forgiveness. Every night spend some time thinking through your day and if you find anyone in need of your forgiveness offer it to them freely. Also, ask for forgiveness if you realize that you have fallen short. This daily practice of extending and receiving forgiveness will help us to go to bed with a light heart and a clear mind.

Day 27: Thoughts of a Realist

Have you ever met a person that always looked on the bad side no matter what was presented to them? They're the type of people that could find the dark cloud on a beautiful sunny day, or the problem in every solution. Are you that person? When we are the type of person that always seeks out the negative or we are around people like that, it can make it hard for us to believe the promises of God, especially when we find ourselves facing challenges on our Christian journey.

The Bible's solution for this is for us to train our minds to think on good things. In Philippians 4:8-9, we are taught to think on things that are pure, lovely, and admirable and the such. Most importantly, in this list of descriptions, we are charged to think on things that are, above all, true.

You see, most of the people that focus on the negative try to cover their pessimistic attitude by claiming that they're realists, but those that choose to focus on the good in the world, are just as much of a realist as their counterparts. So what kind of realist will you be? Will you focus on the negative realities that we all know exist and that can often stifle our ability to hope and bring change, or will you be the type of realist that lets the beauty of the world motivate you to add more beauty to it?

Take a moment and write a few thoughts on the type of realist that you are and how it has impacted the way that you view the world. If you find yourself on the negative side of things, write down 1-2 ways you can move to the more positive thought process.

_____
_____
_____
_____
_____
_____
_____

Day 28: There's Levels To This

In your journey as a Christian, you will never arrive to a place where you learned all that there is to learn on this side of eternity. Whether you've been a Christian for one day or 100 years, there is always an opportunity for you to grow in your faith and go to the next level. In 2 Peter 1:5-9, we are given this list of attributes like brotherly love, self-control and the like to make sure that we add to our life as we grow in our faith. And even when the writer gets to the end of the list, we are encouraged to keep adding even more of these attributes to make it to the next level. This is our friendly reminder that there is always room for growth on this faith journey. And if we choose not to keep growing we will become ineffective in our ministry. God is taking every opportunity to make us more like His son Jesus, and if we are open to it we will find ourselves on an amazing adventure.

CHALLENGE: Read the list of attributes that are listed in 2 Peter 1:5-9. Which one of these areas do you need the most help in adding to your life? List three things that you can do to help your faith grow in that area and practice those three things over the next week.

Growth Area: _____

1. _____
2. _____
3. _____

Day 29: Baptism

Have you ever joined a club or organizations that had a way of publicly acknowledging new members? Maybe they hosted a party in your honor or put your picture up on a wall. Maybe they gave you a shirt or a pin or some other kind of paraphernalia so that other people knew that you were a member of their organization. In Christianity, the special party or welcoming ceremony is called a baptism. It's a way to publicly celebrate the private decision that you made to accept Jesus as your Lord and Savior. It lets everyone know that you've decided to join His team, and it lets people know that you want to be associated with His family. In Acts 22:16, we are told to not delay in asking for forgiveness of our sins and being baptized which symbolically cleanses them away. It's another sign that we've made a fresh start with Christ and a truly special milestone in our Christian journey!

CHALLENGE: If you have not done so already, speak with your youth leader about what you need to do to be baptized in your church. Share your decision for baptism with your family and friends and invite them all to join you in celebrating this amazing faith milestone.

If you still have some questions about baptism and are not quite yet ready to make this public declaration, share your questions with your youth leader, and work together to get the answers that you need to make a sound decision.

It's a big deal in our faith and a cause for great celebration!

Day 30: What Next?

Have you ever seen a movie or heard a story so good that you had to go out and share it with your friends? In hearing the story of Jesus Christ and accepting Him as your savior, you have now not only heard, but also taken part in the greatest story ever told. The best part about it, is that this story is absolutely true! Our natural response to this truth, should be that we now personalize this story, and take the time to share it with others in our lives that haven't heard it in a way that they can fully understand it. We do this so that they can experience the same awesomeness that we now have in our lives. And this is why Jesus gives us the Great Commission.

At the end of Matthew 28 after the resurrection, Jesus tells his followers to go and make more followers, also known as disciples, all over the world! He has given them this life altering message and He gives them the responsibility to make sure that everyone has access to it. Because they were faithful to the assignment, you are here today, over 2000 years later, hearing the same life changing message and responding to it. It is now your responsibility as a disciple of Jesus Christ, to share this message with others.

Also, later in Romans 10:13, Paul says, "Everyone who calls on the name of the Lord will be saved. But how can they call on him to save them unless they believe in him? And how can they believe in him if they have never heard about him? And how can they hear about him unless someone tells them? [15] And how will anyone go and tell them without being sent? That is why the Scriptures say, 'How beautiful are the feet of messengers who bring good news!'"

As a new believer you are now being sent back into your families, your schools, and your communities to share the message that you have so graciously received. You are the messengers with the beautiful feet sharing the good news that Jesus lived, Jesus died, and Jesus lives again and because of this we all can live with Him in this life, and for eternity in the next if we accept the saving grace that He offers us through salvation.

You are encouraged to take this assignment seriously as it was one of the final things that Jesus gave to His followers before ascending into heaven. Take every opportunity to share this good news with those that you meet in your daily life, and to add more disciples to the Kingdom and members to our heavenly family.

CHALLENGE: Identify 10 people that you want to share this good news with over the next month. It is not up to you to make them accept Christ. That is a job for the Holy Spirit. However, it is your responsibility to make sure that they at least hear the message that could change their life forever, just like it changed yours. You can share your personal story or invite them to church with you to hear the Good News of Jesus Christ.

1. _____
2. _____
3. _____
4. _____
5. _____
6. _____
7. _____
8. _____
9. _____
10. _____

NOTE: Sharing your faith can be a scary thing, especially if it's your first time doing so, but know that you are not in this alone. If you are feeling nervous about this assignment, or you think you don't really know what to say, reach out to your youth leader or one of your accountability partners to help you develop a game plan. They'll be more than willing to help you complete this challenge.

The End...And the Beginning

IT IS FINISHED!

Thank you so much for allowing us to guide you through this amazing time at the beginning of your Christian journey. We pray that this guide was helpful as you start your new life in Christ. We are excited about everything that you have learned and the ways that God has been able to reveal more of Himself to you over the last 30 days. We pray that you feel more equipped and confident in your ability to walk out your faith journey and that you are reminded that you are not in this alone. With God, Jesus, the Holy Spirit, your family and your faith community, there is no challenge that is too great for you to face, no question too difficult to be answered, and no purpose too big to be accomplished.

IT IS JUST BEGINNING!

As mentioned throughout the devotional, your faith journey is FAR from over. You are just getting started on what is sure to be one of, if not the most amazing adventure of your life. Share some of the things that meant the most to you over the last 30 days with your small group or your youth leader. Share what you're excited about for the days to come. Let them know where you have grown and where you still need to grow. Share your insights and most importantly, ask your questions. As we shared on Day 3, this Christian experience is meant to be lived out in community, so make sure that you invite your community into your life!

Again, we are so excited for you! Continue to write your story and watch God work in and through your life in ways that you never thought possible!

GO!

Adventure Awaits!

Made in the USA
Lexington, KY
02 December 2018